Sparrows
Pack 4
Jo Apperley

Teaching Notes

Co...
Intro...
Voca...
Curr...

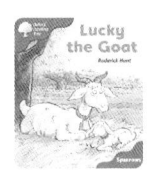

Lucky the Goat

Reading	6
Comprehension	7
Speaking and listening	8
Writing	8

Yasmin and the Flood

Reading	9
Comprehension	10
Speaking and listening	11
Writing	11

Mosque School

Reading	12
Comprehension	13
Speaking and listening	14
Writing	14

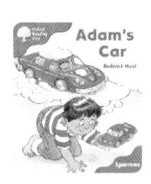

Adam's Car

Reading	15
Comprehension	16
Speaking and listening	17
Writing	17

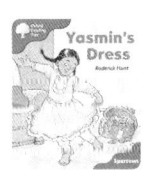

Yasmin's Dress

Reading	18
Comprehension	20
Speaking and listening	20
Writing	20

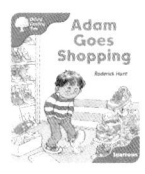

Adam Goes Shopping

Reading	21
Comprehension	22
Speaking and listening	23
Writing	23

Links to other Oxford Reading Tree titles   24

Introduction

The Sparrows stories at Stage 4 provide consolidation for children who need plenty of practice before moving to the next stage. The stories are at the same level of difficulty as the other stories at Stage 4. The same key words and high frequency words are used. New nouns and verbs are usually obvious from the illustrations.

Sparrows introduce new characters and new settings , broadening the children's reading base. These stories do not include Biff, Chip and Kipper.

To help children approach each new book in this stage with confidence, prepare the children for reading by talking about the book, asking questions and using the support material to introduce new characters and settings.

As children read these stories they are encouraged to read independently through: using their knowledge of letter sounds; learning to recognise high frequency words on sight; using the pictures and the sense of the story to work out new vocabulary, with less reliance on picture cues.

How to introduce the books

Before reading the story, it is still important to talk about the picture on the cover. Go through the book together, looking at the pictures and talking about them. If there are context words (listed in the chart on page 4 of this booklet) that are new or unfamiliar, point them out and read them with the children. While they read the story, encourage the children to scan whole sentences before reading and to finger point only when working out particular words.

This booklet provides suggestions for using the books in group and independent activities. Prompts and ideas are provided for introducing and reading each book with a child or group of children. Suggestions are also provided for writing, speaking and listening and cross-curricular links. You can use these suggestions to follow on from your reading, or use at another time.

Take-Home Cards are also available for each book. These provide friendly prompts and suggestions for parents reading with their children. You can store the relevant card with each book in your "Take-Home" selection of titles.

Reading skills

Stage 4 develops:
- confidence in reading longer texts
- the ability to sustain a story from one book to another
- the ability to understand more complex plots within a book
- the ability to be more reflective about reading
- the use of strategies to check the sense of the text
- growing confidence in writing independently.

Vocabulary chart

Lucky the Goat	**Years 1 to 2 High frequency words** after back called every gave had have her over two with
	Context words aeroplane chicken pox couldn't doctor everyone goat grandmother holiday kid looked lucky party played sad spots stayed wanted weeks
Yasmin and the Flood	**Years 1 to 2 High frequency words** came have help her out she took what
	Context words cloth couldn't downstairs dry everyone everything flooded hang happy helped lovely let's mess outside party rain shop sleep sun wet woke
Mosque School	**Years 1 to 2 High frequency words** but called came got help his little out ran school too
	Context words climbed couldn't everyone firemen grandad hooray inside lamp mosque post stuck wanted
Adam's Car	**Years 1 to 2 High frequency words** had new over put saw
	Context words bin car couldn't cross dropped everywhere fell find flour idea sorry television
Yasmin's Dress	**Years 1 to 2 High frequency words** got had her his made new off our put what
	Context words cross dress everyone gran's grandfather hands it's looked paint pretty secret upset
Adam Goes Shopping	**Years 1 to 2 High frequency words** him home some took
	Context words asleep bored couldn't everyone fast fed find into kettle shoes suit tent tired track wanted

Curriculum coverage chart

	Speaking and listening	Reading	Writing
Lucky the Goat			
NLS/NC	1f, 4a, 11b	W3, S1, S3, T7	T14
Scotland	Level A/B	Level A/B	Level A/B
N. Ireland	Activities: b, c Outcomes: b, d, e, g	Activities: b, f, h Outcomes: d, f, g	Outcomes: b, c, h
Wales	Range: 5, 6 Skill: 1, 2	Range: 4, 5, 6 Skill: 1, 2	Range: 1, 3, 6 Skill: 2, 6, 7
Yasmin and the Flood			
NLS/NC	4b, 4c	W3, W7, S4, T2, T10	T12
Scotland	Level A/B	Level A/B	Level A/B
N. Ireland	Activities: b, c, f Outcomes: d, e, g	Activities: c, e, f Outcomes: d, e, f	Outcomes: b, c, h, i
Wales	Range: 1, 5, 6 Skill: 2, 5	Range: 2, 5, 6 Skill: 1, 2	Range: 1, 3, 5 Skill: 6, 8
Mosque School			
NLS/NC	2c, 2e, 3b, 9b	W4, S1, S6, T4	T16
Scotland	Level A/B	Level A/B	Level A/B
N. Ireland	Activities: a, f Outcomes: c, g	Activities: a, c Outcomes: b, d, f	Outcomes: e, f, h, l
Wales	Range: 1, 3 Skill: 2, 5	Range: 5, 6 Skill: 1, 2	Range: 3, 7 Skill: 1, 6, 7
Adam's Car			
NLS/NC	1a, 1e, 2b	W6, S4, T8	S5
Scotland	Level A/B	Level A/B	Level A/B
N. Ireland	Activities: f, g, i Outcomes: a, b, e	Activities: c, f Outcomes: c, e, f	Outcomes: c, f, h
Wales	Range: 1, 2 Skill: 1, 2	Range: 4, 5 Skill: 1, 2	Range: 6, 7 Skill: 1, 7, 9
Yasmin's Dress			
NLS/NC	3c, 3e	W2, W6, S1, T7, T9	S7
Scotland	Level A/B	Level A/B	Level A/B
N. Ireland	Activities: f, g Outcomes: a, c, d	Activities: b, f, h Outcomes: b, d, e, f	Outcomes: c, h, i
Wales	Range: 2, 3 Skill: 1, 2, 3	Range: 4, 5 Skill: 1, 2	Range: 2, 3, 4 Skill: 1, 6, 7
Adam Goes Shopping			
NLS/NC	4b, 11a	W7, S1, T2, T4	T15
Scotland	Level A/B	Level A/B	Level A/B
N. Ireland	Activities: b, c Outcomes: a, d, g	Activities: b, f Outcomes: b, d, e	Outcomes: b, f, i
Wales	Range: 5, 6 Skill: 1, 2	Range: 2, 5 Skill: 1, 2	Range: 3, 4, 7 Skill: 1, 2, 8, 9

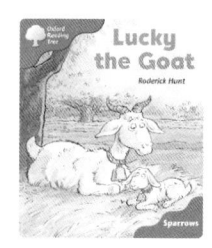

Lucky the Goat

Before reading

- Look at the front cover and encourage the children to read the title.
- Discuss the animal on the front cover and introduce the word "kid" as a baby goat. Ask the children: *How did Yasmin get a goat?* Encourage them to skim through the book for the answer.
- Look at the word "Lucky" and ask the children to describe its meaning.

During reading

- Encourage the children to read the story.
- Praise the children who take time to look at the illustrations and then read the sentence. Re-read a sentence just as the child did if it did not make sense. Ask: *Does that make sense?* Encourage them to try reading it again.
- Encourage the children to blend the phonemes in words with clusters, e.g. "pl-ay-ed", "sp-o-t-s".

Observing Check that the children:

- expect reading to make sense and check if it does not, and read aloud using expression appropriate to the grammar of the text (Y1T2 S1)
- blend phonemes in words with clusters for reading (Y1T2 W3).

Group and independent reading activities

Text level work

Objective To discuss reasons for, or causes of, incidents in stories (Y1T2 T7).

- Ask the children to recap the key events of the story. Prompt them to give reasons why events were happening (e.g. ask: *Why was Yasmin with her grandmother? Why did Grandmother have a party? Why did Adam have spots?*).
- Encourage the children to refer to the text to help them with their answers.

Observing Can the children give reasons for key events in the story?

Sentence level work

Objective To predict words from preceding words in sentences and investigate the sorts of words that "fit", suggesting appropriate alternatives (Y1T2 S3).

- Turn to pages 8 and 9. Read the first part of sentence: *"Yasmin looked after ..."*. Encourage the children to describe an alternative word to "Lucky" that would also fit. Discuss their suggestions.
- Prompt the children to question whether these suggestions make sense and don't change the meaning.
- Repeat for the other sentences on these pages.

Observing Can the children think of alternative words that make sense?

Word level work

Objective To blend phonemes in words with clusters for reading (Y1T2 W3).
- Discuss with the children how you can blend phonemes together.
- Encourage them to look through the text and find examples of when phonemes have been blended together to make new sounds.

Observing Can the children find examples of blended phonemes in the text?

Comprehension

Ask the children:
- *How did they go on holiday?* (p1 They went by aeroplane.)
- *How did they get to Grandmother's house?* (p2 by taxi)
- *What is a kid?* (a baby goat)
- *On page 11, why is Yasmin sad?* (She doesn't want to leave Lucky.)
- *On page 15, why did the doctor say "Come back in two weeks"?* (Adam's chicken pox would be better, and they would be able to fly home.)

Lucky the Goat

Speaking and listening activities

Objectives Take into account the needs of their listeners (1f); use language and actions to explore and convey situations, characters and emotions (4a); present drama and stories to others (11b).

- Ask the children to re-enact the story and encourage them to expand key events in the story (e.g. at the airport or at the party).
- Encourage them to think how the key characters might have behaved and what they may have said.

◀▶ Cross-curricular links
D&T: moving pictures
Geography: Where in the World is Barnaby Bear?

Writing

Objective To represent outlines of story plots using, e.g. captions, pictures, arrows to record main incidents in order (Y1T2 T14).

- Discuss with the children the concept of a wall story.
- Explain to them that you would like them to retell the story of "Lucky the Goat" but only using six pages. Encourage them to plan the layout and decide what text and which illustration should go on each page.
- Remind the children that they are working together as a group and producing one story outline and not six story outlines.

Yasmin and the Flood

Before reading

- Read the title with the children and ask the children: *What do you think has happened?*
- Look on pages 4 and 5 and discuss where Yasmin is. (She is in her house at the back of her parents' shop.)
- Look through the book together and introduce new or difficult words while talking about what Yasmin and her family are doing.

During reading

- Ask the children to read the story. Praise and encourage them while they read and prompt as necessary.
- When necessary, discuss and introduce new phonemes to help the children decipher new words (e.g. "r<u>ai</u>n," "fl<u>oo</u>ded", "p<u>ar</u>ty").
- Encourage the children to predict the context words by using the picture clues and the initial sounds, and by breaking the words into separate words (e.g. "out/side", "every/thing", "down/stairs").

Observing Check that the children:

- use phonological, contextual, grammatical and graphic knowledge to work out, predict and check the meanings of unfamiliar words and to make sense of what they read (Y1T2 T2)
- blend phonemes in words with clusters for reading (Y1T2 W3).

Group and independent reading activities

Text level work

Objective To identify and compare basic story elements, e.g. beginnings and endings in different stories (Y1T2 T10).

- Ask the children to identify and record what happened at the beginning of the story. Encourage them to record the event using pictures and by writing a caption.
- Encourage the children to record what happened at the end of the story, using pictures and a caption.

- Repeat the terms "beginning" and "ending", asking the children to hold up the appropriate drawings. Discuss other familiar stories and ask the children to describe their beginnings and endings.

Observing Can the children identify the beginnings and endings in familiar stories?

Sentence level work

Objective To recognise full stops and capital letters when reading and understand how they affect the way a passage is read (Y1T2 S4).

- Read the story again but without pausing and stopping at full stops.
- Ask the children: *What was wrong with the way I read the story? What should I have done?*
- Ask the children to find the full stops on each page and demonstrate how the page should be read.

Observing Can the children understand and apply their knowledge of full stops to their reading?

Word level work

Objective To recognise the critical features of words, e.g. length, common spelling patterns and words within words (Y1T2 W7).

- Turn to page 2 and ask the children to look at the word "downstairs". Ask: *What do you notice about this word?* Praise the children who notice that it is made of two words.
- Ask the children to find other examples in the text where two words have been joined to make a new word ("Everything", "outside", "Everyone").

Observing Can the children find words within words?

Comprehension

Ask the children:
- *On page 1, why did the rain wake Yasmin up?* (the sound)
- *On page 3, what did Yasmin discover downstairs?* (the flood)
- *On page 6, what is Mum carrying?* (cloth)
- *Why did Yasmin think hanging up the fabrics would help?* (p11 It would help it dry.)

Yasmin and the Flood

- *How did they hang up the fabric?* (pp12–13 Everyone helped to hang it across the street, from window to window.)

Speaking and listening activities

Objectives Create and sustain roles individually and when working with others (4b); comment constructively on drama they have watched or in which they have taken part (4c).

- Tell the children to imagine they arrive at school one day and find their classroom flooded. Ask them to work in pairs, deciding what they might do and how they might react. Encourage them to present the event as a play.
- Encourage them to act out the play in front of the other children and ask the others to contribute their thoughts and feelings once their sketch is complete.
- Prompt the children to be sensitive to the needs of other children and how they may feel about criticism.

◀▶ **Cross-curricular links**
Art: investigating materials
Science: sorting and using materials

Writing

Objective Through shared and guided writing, apply phonological, graphic knowledge and sight vocabulary to spell words accurately (Y1T2 T12).

- Show the children the front cover of a newspaper.
- Ask the children to work together in pairs to create a front cover for a local newspaper describing the terrible floods. Prompt them to write it in draft first and apply their phonological, graphic knowledge and sight vocabulary to spell words accurately.
- Give them plenty of time to illustrate and write headings for their newspapers.
- Encourage them to type the final text on a computer, print it out and combine it with the illustrations to complete the front cover.

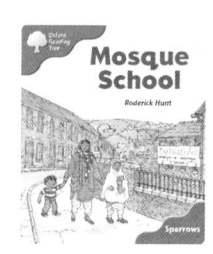

Mosque School

Before reading

- Ask: *Do you recognise any words in the title?* Praise the children who recognise the term "school".
- Read the term "Mosque" to the children and encourage them to repeat it after you. Discuss how a Mosque school is a place where Islamic children can go to learn after school and at the weekend.

During reading

- Ask the children to read the story. Praise and encourage them while they read, and prompt as necessary.
- As you listen, check the children understand the grammar in the text and read appropriately.
- Ensure the children are reading high frequency words ("school", "but", "too", "little", "got", "his", "called", "help", "ran", "came", "out") without hesitation or any prompting.

Observing Check that the children:

- read aloud using expression appropriate to the grammar of the text (Y1T2 S1)
- read on sight high frequency words specific to graded reading books matched to the abilities of reading groups (Y1T2 W4).

Group and independent reading activities

Text level work

Objective To retell stories, giving the main points in sequence and to notice differences between written and spoken forms in retelling, e.g. by comparing oral versions with the written text; to refer to relevant phrases and sentences (Y1T2 T4).

- Ask the children, individually, to retell the story and prompt them to notice the differences between what they are describing and what is written in the text.
- Remind the children to retell the story in the right order and to try not to miss out any key events.

Observing Can the children retell the story, giving the main points in sequence without prompting?

Sentence level work

Objective To use the term "sentence" appropriately to identify sentences in text, i.e. those demarcated by capital letters and full stops (Y1T2 S6).

- Ask: *How many sentences can you find in the book?* (14) Prompt the children by asking: *What are the key features of a sentence that we should be looking for?*
- Turn to pages 1 and 15. Discuss with the children the difference between a line and a sentence. Ask: *How many lines are in this book?*

Observing Can the children identify the sentences in the book?

Word level work

Objective For guided reading to read on sight high frequency words specific to graded reading books matched to the abilities of reading groups (Y1T2 W4).

- Ask: *Can you find the word "but" in the book?* (p3) Praise children for skimming through the text to find the word.
- Ask: *How many times are the words "help" and "school" used in the book?* (Both are used twice.) Encourage the children to record their findings in a simple table.
- Demonstrate reading the following high frequency words, using phonological knowledge and not sight knowledge: "school", "but", "too", "little", "got", "his", "called", "help", "ran", "came", "out". Remind the children that these words and others can be read straight away and there is no need to sound them out.

Observing Can the children identify high frequency words in the text?

Comprehension

Ask the children:
- *Who goes to a mosque school?* (p1 Yasmin)
- *Why did Adam climb on the lamp post?* (p6 He couldn't see inside the school.)

- *How did Adam get stuck behind the lamp post?* (p8 He got stuck between the wall and the lamp post.)
- *On page 11, who is the man phoning in the phone booth?* (the firemen)
- *How did the firemen get Adam out?* (p12 illustration: They pulled the lamp post away from the wall.)

Speaking and listening activities

Objectives Make relevant comments (2c); ask questions to clarify their understanding (2e); relate their contributions to what has gone on before (3b); listen to adults giving detailed explanations and presentations (9b).

- Read some information books about Islam and Islamic mosques to the children. Describe the key features of Islam.
- Prompt the children to make relevant comments during the reading. Encourage any Islamic children in the class to tell the other children about their religion.
- Discuss as a group the information just heard and encourage the children to ask questions about Islam.

◀▶ Cross-curricular links
D&T: homes
RE: beliefs and practice

Writing

Objective To use some of the elements of known stories to structure own writing (Y1T2 T16).

- Recap with the children the key events from the story (Adam wanting to go to school; Adam climbing the lamp post; Adam getting stuck; Adam being rescued; Adam being allowed to go to school).
- Ask the children to write their own story, remembering the key events. Check that they include background information/scene setting, the event, and the solution/ending.

Adam's Car

Before reading

- Read the title with the children and discuss the apostrophe "s" in the word "Adam's". Explain that it is not a plural (lots of Adams) but that it tells us that the car belongs to Adam.
- Look carefully at the front cover and ask the children: *Can you find the same illustration in the book?* (p5) Discuss how Adam is using his imagination to imagine he is driving the car.
- Ask: *Where is Adam imagining he is driving the car? What setting is he imagining?*

During reading

- Ask the children to read the story. Praise and encourage them to decode words when necessary but also to recognise on sight words such as: "had", "new", "saw", "put", "over".
- Periodically ask the children to point out the full stops and capital letters on the page they are reading.

Observing Check that the children:

- recognise full stops and capital letters when reading and understand how they affect the way a passage is read (Y1 T 2 S4)
- read on sight more high frequency words (Y1T2 W6).

Group and independent reading activities

Text level work

Objective To identify and discuss characters, e.g. appearance, behaviour, qualities; to speculate about how they might behave (Y1T2 T8).

- Discuss what sort of character Adam is. Encourage the children to describe key features to each other, and together create a list of his appearance, behaviour, etc.
- Ask: *Do you think Adam is a well-behaved boy or a naughty boy?* Ask the children to give reasons for their answers.

Observing Can the children identify and name key characteristics about Adam?

Sentence level work

Objective To recognise full stops and capital letters when reading and understand how they affect the way a passage is read (Y1T2 S4).

- Discuss with the children how they would have to read the passage if the full stops were not there. Encourage them to demonstrate.
- Ask: *What other punctuation helps us to know how to read a sentence?* (speech marks, commas, exclamation marks, etc.)

Observing Can the children demonstrate an understanding of how full stops affect the way a passage is read?

Word level work

Objective To read on sight high frequency words (Y1T2 W6).

- Turn to page 2. Read the sentence on page 2 and decode each word in turn. Discuss with the children how this method of reading sounds. Ask: *What can be done to make it sound better?*
- Talk to the children about re-reading sentences they have just decoded and using their sight vocabulary to help them read more fluently.
- Ask them to look through the text and find the words: "had", "new", "saw", "put", "over". Discuss how they appear frequently not only in this book but in other books too, and so are useful words to recognise quickly and not have to decode.

Observing Can the children find key words in the text?

Comprehension

Ask the children:
- *On page 3, what is the car on the television doing?* (Racing down a snowy slope.)
- *On page 5, what is Adam's idea?* (That he can race in the snow in his car, too.)

Adam's Car

- *On page 7, why is Adam putting flour on the car?* (To look like snow.)
- *On page 11, why could Adam not find his car?* (It is lost in the flour.)
- *On page 16, who is tidying up the mess?* (Adam and his mum.)

Speaking and listening activities

Objectives Speak with clear diction and appropriate intonation (1a); include relevant detail (1e), remember specific points that interest them (2b).

- Ask each child, individually, to retell the story. Encourage them to remember key events and relevant details.
- Encourage the children to retell the story into a tape recorder. Give them time to prepare so that they can tell the story without your support or any prompting. Remind them to speak clearly.

Cross-curricular links
Art: What is Sculpture?
Science: pushes and pulls

Writing

Objective To continue demarcating sentences in writing, ending a sentence with a full stop (Y1T2 S5).

- Ask the children to write about a time when their mum or dad was cross because of something they did.
- Encourage the children to explain what they did wrong, why it was wrong, how their parents reacted and how the problem was fixed.
- Prompt them to include full stops in their writing and to encourage them to re-read their writing to check they have been included.

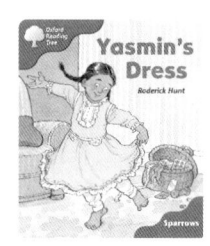

Yasmin's Dress

Before reading

- Show the children the cover. Ask the children: *What do you think Mum is doing? What is Yasmin doing? How is Yasmin feeling?*
- Read the title with the children and ask: *Where did Yasmin's dress come from?*
- Turn to page 1 and find clues to help us work out where Yasmin's dress came from.

During reading

- Ask the children to read the story. Praise and encourage them to read fluently and with expression.
- As you listen, ask the children to point to the words that characters say and identify the punctuation marks.
- Encourage the children to read on sight high frequency words ("had", "new", "put", "what", "got", "his", "made", "her", "off", "our") and prompt them not to decode the words or use other strategies.

Observing Check that the children:

- are becoming increasingly aware of character and dialogue, e.g. by role-playing parts when reading aloud stories or plays with others (Y1T2 T9)
- read on sight approximately 30 more high frequency words (Y1T2 W6).

Group and independent reading activities

Text level work

Objective To discuss reasons for, or causes of, incidents in stories (Y1T2 T7).

- Turn to pages 12–13. Discuss how the children are feeling and encourage them to use a variety of different adjectives (e.g. sad, disappointed, embarrassed, ashamed, angry, mad).

- Ask: *Do you think Yasmin was right to be cross?* and prompt them to give reasons for their answers. Ask: *Do you think Adam was right to be upset?* and prompt them to give reasons for their answers.

Observing Can the children relate the feelings of the characters to the incidents that occurred in the book?

Sentence level work

Objective To read aloud using expression appropriate to the grammar of the text (Y1T2 S1).

- On page 11, encourage the children in turn to read what Yasmin says. Discuss how each person read the text and what feelings they portray in their reading.
- Encourage the children to think about how Yasmin might be feeling and prompt them to read again, using the appropriate expression.
- Repeat for page 16, encouraging the children to read with expression what grandfather said and to explain to the group how they think he felt.

Observing Can the children read aloud, taking into consideration the feelings and expressions of the characters?

Word level work

Objective To investigate, read and spell words ending in "ss" (Y1T2 W2).

- Look at the title. Ask: *What do you notice about the word "dress"?* Discuss how it has the ending "ss".
- Encourage the children to look through the text for another word with the "ss" ending (p12 "cross"). Create a list with the children of other words that end in "ss".

Observing Can the children recognise and spell words with the "ss" ending?

Comprehension

Ask the children:
- *How did Mum make Yasmin's dress?* (p3 with a sewing machine)
- *How do we know that the paint is wet in the playground?* (p9 "wet paint" sign)
- *On page 13, why was Adam upset?* (He got paint on Yasmin's dress and made her cross.)
- *How did Grandfather get the paint out of Yasmin's dress?* (p14 illustration: With a bottle of liquid from the shed.)
- *On page 16, why did Grandfather want to keep it all a secret?* (So that Adam didn't get into trouble.)

Speaking and listening activities

Objective Take different views into account (3c); give reasons for opinions and actions (3e).

- Talk about Yasmin's dress with the children. Ask: *Do you agree or disagree that it is a pretty dress?* Encourage them to give reasons for their answers.
- Prompt them to respond to each other's differing opinions and to take them into account when giving their answers.

◀▶ Cross-curricular links
D&T: playgrounds
Science: sorting and using materials

Writing

Objective To use capital letters for the personal pronoun 'I', for names and for the start of a sentence (Y1T2 S7).

- Discuss with the children a new item they have that may have got broken or damaged. Encourage them to recount how the item got broken and how it made them feel.
- Prompt them to use capital letters for the personal pronoun "I".

Adam Goes Shopping

Before reading

- Read the title and look at the illustration. Ask the children: *How is Adam feeling?*
- Look through the book and discuss how Adam is feeling on each page.
- Look at page 7 and introduce the word "bored" to the children. Encourage them to find the word in the text. Discuss why Adam might be feeling bored in the story.

During reading

- Ask the children to read the story. Praise and encourage them while they read, and prompt as necessary.
- Check the children can read the ending "–ed": "wanted", "bored", "tired", "looked".
- Periodically ask the children to explain how they are decoding and deciphering new words. Remind the children to re-read sentences to ensure fluency once they have decoded the words.

Observing Check that the children:

- use phonological, contextual, grammatical and graphic knowledge to work out, predict and check the meaning of unfamiliar words and to make sense of what they read (Y1T2 T2)
- recognise the critical features of words, e.g. length, common spelling patterns (Y1T2 W7).

Group and independent reading activities

Text level work

Objective To retell stories, giving the main points in sequence and to notice differences between written and spoken forms in retelling (Y1T2 T4).

- Ask the children to retell what happened in the story. Prompt them to refer to words used in the text (e.g. "bored", "tired", "fed up").

- Remind the children to retell the story in sequence to prevent omitting key points.

Observing Can the children retell the story in detail and in sequence?

Sentence level work

Objective To expect reading to make sense and check if it does not, and to read aloud using expression appropriate to the grammar of the text (Y1T2 S1).

- Turn to page 1. Look at the ending of the word "shopping". Ask the children to cover the "–ing" ending and read the sentence again. Ask: *Does it make sense?*
- Encourage the children to say "–ed" at the end of the word and ask again: *Does that make sense?*
- Discuss how words are written down to make sense and how it is important that we read the whole word and not just the initial part.

Observing Can the children hear when a sentence does not make sense?

Word level work

Objective To recognise the critical features of words (Y1T2 W7).

- Look through the story together and create two lists of words with endings "–ing", and "–ed". Read the list through together and discuss how each ending affects the words ("–ing" creates actions/"doing" words; "–ed" words are to do with the past/"was" words).
- Encourage the children to think of other words to add to the lists.

Observing Can the children find and recognise "–ing" and "–ed" endings?

Comprehension

Ask the children:
- *On page 3, how is Adam feeling?* (bored)
- *On page 6, why doesn't Yasmin want to go home?* (She wants some shoes.)

Adam Goes Shopping

- *On page 7, what kind of shoes is the man trying on and why?* (Funny shoes, probably because he is a clown.)
- *On page 8, what kind of shop are they in?* (sports shop)
- *On page 15, why can't they find Adam?* (He is in the tent.)

Speaking and listening activities

Objectives Create and sustain roles individually and when working with others (4b); work in role (11a).

- Ask the children to work in small groups and retell the story of "Adam Goes Shopping".
- Prompt them to use their facial expressions to communicate how everyone in the family is feeling throughout the story.

Cross-curricular links
Art: self-portraits
Numeracy: money

Writing

Objective To build simple profiles of characters from stories read, describing characteristics, appearances, behaviour with pictures, single words, captions, words and sentences from text (Y1T2 T15).

- Ask the children to choose a character from the story and create a character profile for a poster.
- Encourage them to draw their character in the centre of a page and write key behaviour displayed in the story. Prompt them to use the text to help them with their spelling of key words.
- Remind the children they can write labels instead of sentences.

Oxford Reading Tree resources at this level

Stage 4

Teacher support
- Teacher's Handbook
- Big Talkabout Cards
- Big Books for Stage 4 Stories
- Guided Reading Cards for Stage 4 Stories
- Take-Home Card for each story
- Extended Stories
- Storytapes / More Storytapes
- Word Cards
- Context Cards
- Workbooks 4a and 4b
- Woodpeckers Introductory Phonic Workbooks C and D
- Sequencing Cards Photocopy Masters
- Group Activity Sheets Book 2 Stage 4-5
- ORT Games Stages 4 and 5

Further reading
- Stage 4 Playscripts
- Fireflies Non-Fiction
- Fact Finders Units A, B and C
- Acorns and More Acorns Poetry

Electronic
- Clip Art
- Stage 4 Talking Stories
- ORT Online www.OxfordReadingTree.com
- Floppy and Friends

For developing phonics
- Alphabet frieze, Tabletop Alphabet Mats, Alphabet Photocopy Masters
- Card Games
- Story Rhymes

OXFORD
UNIVERSITY PRESS

Great Clarendon Street, Oxford OX2 6DP

Oxford University Press is a department of the University of Oxford. It furthers the University's objective of excellence in research, scholarship, and education by publishing worldwide in

Oxford New York

Auckland Cape Town Dar es Salaam Hong Kong Karachi Kuala Lumpur Madrid Melbourne Mexico City Nairobi New Delhi Shanghai Taipei Toronto

With offices in

Argentina Austria Brazil Chile Czech Republic France Greece Guatemala Hungary Italy Japan Poland Portugal Singapore South Korea Switzerland Thailand Turkey Ukraine Vietnam

Oxford is a registered trade mark of Oxford University Press in the UK and in certain other countries

© Oxford University Press 2003

The moral rights of the author have been asserted

Database right Oxford University Press (maker)

First published 2003

All rights reserved. No part of this publication may be reproduced, stored in a retrieval system, or transmitted, in any form or by any means, without the prior permission in writing of Oxford University Press, or as expressly permitted by law, or under terms agreed with the appropriate reprographics rights organization. Enquiries concerning reproduction outside the scope of the above should be sent to the Rights Department, Oxford University Press, at the address above

You must not circulate this book in any other binding or cover and you must impose this same condition on any acquirer

British Library Cataloguing in Publication Data

Data available

Cover artwork by David Parkins

Teacher's Notes: ISBN 978-0-19-845400-7

10

Page make-up by IFA Design Ltd, Plymouth, Devon

Printed in China by Imago